Naked & True
Volume 1

SD Johnson

© 2020 by SD Johnson

All rights reserved. No part of this publication may be reproduced, distributed, or transmitted in any form by any means, including photocopying, recording, or other electronic methods without the prior written permission of the author, except in the case of brief quotations embodied in reviews and certain other noncommercial uses permitted by copyright law.

Cover design & layout: KDP Amazon
Author Photo: J Shon Holifield for J Shon Digital Media

ISBN: 9781655297441
Printed in the United States of America
2020, May 27

For my mother,
Tondalayo P. Dodd

Because of you, I am one...one of me
And without you, I became lost
But your spirit found me and now I live

Before the Storm

Clouds are dangerous
As they block out the light
The light that once shined bright
The sun has run away
Hiding in the distance
Pretending to care
But all of the glory cannot be bright

The calm is just the beginning
Tragedy grips the soul
As silence frightens the mind
The body is trembling, no control
So loud and so cruel
So demanding and so rude
No one is safe

The cycle of pain continues
It's always present
When the storm comes through

The calm is just the beginning
As the tsunami of death plagues
The human heart

With every single beat, the heart
doesn't stop…before the storm, there
was peace

MOTHERHOOD

Miracle

I woke up to a beautiful blessing
Her tiny eyes watching me with ease
Her sweet baby noises gave me life
As I have given unto her
Her smile was brief before she yawned
The sunlight kissed her soft face
And when she cried, I found no peace
In wanting her to stop
As I have waited for this sound for so long
As I have waited for that beloved face to look like my own
When she is old enough, I will tell her
About our journey and the struggle within...many nights of tears...
Many nights of hopelessness and depression...many times too much
For what we did not have...until now
And suddenly, it happened
I became bloated with love
I became elated with joy
Carried my first...my tender moment
My sweet, sweet baby girl

Little Heart

So playful – always smiling
Each day is a blessing with her
Each moment is precious
Soft and cuddly
Warm hugs
Soft kisses
The way she calls my name
The way she makes my heart feel
My little one
My sweetest girl

Sweet Baby

Each moment is precious
And she never takes them for granted
Each hour brings her closer
Edging towards the love within
Within these moments
She realizes a truth
She is...a mother...to her sweet baby
Perfect
Loving
Again, and again

Baby No More

So young
Personality shining through
Each moment and each day
So special with you

Test momma's patience
Spoil you rotten
You resemble your dad
He's a great father

Momma birthed you
And you latched on tight
Stealing her energy
Many sleepless nights

Growing so quickly
Momma can't keep up
Not ready for the future
Of you all grown up

At last, momma's sweet baby girl
Momma's heart and soul
Time should slow down
Momma wants more time
To hold onto you a little longer

FAMILY

Momma

It has been too many years
Too many thoughts
Too many tears
I need to hear your voice
Loud and clear
Through the rain
      The storm
      The thunder
      The lightning with spheres
Too many days without you here
I want to see you
I need to…it's my only way to unfold
But time will not let me
And I miss you
I miss your hugs and kisses too
I miss being with you
I pray that you are watching me
Waiting
Sitting
      In the place that is eternity

Family Portrait

We tried to call you
But you decided on silence
Estranged from all of us
We cannot find you
You changed your ways
In how you feel about us
We still love you
Even if you have turned a blind eye
We hope that you will talk to us again
If one of us dies
We believe you when your actions speak
We haven't heard from you
Not now – not in a week
You cast us from your life
No understanding
No reason
Just ridiculous strife
We want to see you
And hear your voice
But your actions give us pause
…we have no choice

Daddy Issues

We don't speak
I don't know who you are
And you haven't met the grown version
of me…the adult…the one that you
have yet to see
You used to teach me things
When I was a young girl
And would punish me when I wasn't a
part of your perfect world

Momma pressed on
And so, you were told to leave
Leave before the illness
Took her…to heaven…swiftly

You gave two more your bloodline
And neglected your first two – my
brother and I
Without a care in the world

While so many have their fathers
I sit here wondering why things turned
out the way they did

I have daddy's issues…not hidden but
real…

Dear Brothers

The three of us...inseparable
As children...laughing and playing
Running around
Our toys became our escape
While we reasoned with one another
To behave before trouble found us

Now that we are grown
We find solace in our maturity
Still smiling, laughing, and sometimes
crying

Crying within
Dear brothers, I love you
Miss you
Now and until the end

Brother

You are the youngest of the two of us
A baby...
    Spoiled and rotten
But you are mine

My sibling, my twin, my blood
    All of the time
Our fights are verbal
Sometimes the words sting too much
    Just like a bee
And yet, I love you...unconditionally

We have not spoken in quite some time
And soon it crosses over into years
My heart hurts
My heavy tears

I find relief in knowing that you are okay
Wondering...waiting...this silence is without delay

What would our mother say?
What would she do?
I admit, life is not the same without you

My dear brother, I love and miss you

PERSONAL REFLECTION

My Thoughts

Sometimes it grips my soul
When I think about what life means
And when I cannot cope
I find tranquility in being alone

Sometimes it allows me silence
But it often drags me down
Turning my smile into a frown
Sometimes it angers me
Pushing and shoving
Trying to consume my entire existence

And yet, it will consume me because I am living

Sometimes meditation does not help
Wearing me down
Placing my anguish on a shelf

Sometimes...
My thoughts are too much
Even for me
Too much for my soul
As I am trapped...never free

Revenge

Red – red eyes
Red – red words
    As if color could be shown
    It's not as sweet as they say
    It is harsh – demanding
    Complex – outrage

Red – red eyes
Red – red words
    Threats of violence
    To make the soul whole
    There are no visions
    Of forgiveness
    Not now – not ever

Patience

Sometimes I fight it and curse at it
As I want nothing more than to end it
It catches me off guard
Never allowing me to rest
Disturbing my peace
Beating against my chest
Counting to ten does not slow it down
It becomes impossible
It becomes now
I want no part of it – ever
But I continue to give in
Pretending to care
Pretending again and again
Sometimes I snatch it from my mind
Destroying my space
Disregarding my time
Sometimes…
I could careless that it's not connected to me

Alone

The clock continues to tick
As I sit by the window
Trying to find my peace
While my sanity hangs on

Each moment of silence
Is what makes me hold
Onto myself so tight
In the moment
Quiet…
Nothing moving nor in sight

I want to get up and go
But in this quaint moment,
I need to be alone

Truth

I want to believe you
But the lies are speaking
Talking – telling me the tales
And yet, I cannot hide
What I need from you
Trust
Friendship
And more
I want to wait for you
Hold the door
But the false stories become more
These decrepit lines that you give to me
Breaks my heart and crushes my knees
The nerve of you
Too phony and too fake
Faux thoughts and memories
I want to believe you
        But I can't

Haunted

The lightning has my name written all over it
My fear is driven by the ghosts that haunt me
The ones that linger and circle around my soul
Crippling my peace
Taking back what I once owned
I cannot sleep at night
Each scream deadens me
Each frightening moment holds onto the night
I want to be brave
Take a stand
Show muscle
Show my command
But I am broken
Stretching across the desert
Holding onto the dunes
Sweating
Palpitations
Trying to get back what was stolen from within
I am treading lightly
I am immersed in sin
They taunt me...holding on tight
Stealing my dreams and coming for me at midnight

Rogue

Stand alone or become one of them
You know...the ones that follow
Because they're too afraid to lead

Be brave and speak your mind
Don't mince words
As the truth may sometimes set you free
Hold onto the strength that makes you whole

Give no notice to those who think you have no control
Curse them
Call them what you want
Drive in your own lane
While pushing everyone away

Be confident
Be unapologetic
Be you
Rough and tough
Around the edges
Too sharp to touch
Too hot to hold
Just be...you

Wide Eyes, Dark Mornings

I lay in bed staring at the sun
As it molests my curtains
And I begin to think
Think long and hard about the day before
It was a day that I want to forget
But my eyes continue to see
What was – what should be
Suddenly my doorbell sings
That sweet and subtle tune
All I want is to curl up into my duvet until noon
Ignore all calls
Ignore that doorbell that rings the blues
My mind is warped – tired – exhausted – confused
And I can't move

Black Girl, Black Woman

Sometimes angry
Sometimes not
Shapely – curvy – round in the hips
Sweet and butter-filled
Touch to her sassy lips
Different – never plain
Sometimes impossible
Sometimes sane
Innocent – guilty
Strong and proud
Sometimes quiet
Sometimes too loud
Intelligent – soft – serene
Sometimes intimidating
Sometimes mean
Gracious beings
Sometimes misunderstood
Sometimes…
No, all the time…SHE IS A QUEEN

Threats

You harbor ill will towards me
Whispering angry words
Moaning in agony
As if my pain would ever be weak
You continue to look ahead
And won't acknowledge me
Coward
Respect is gone
You can proceed in your threats
But I won't cower in a corner like a child
But keep fuckin' with me,
I'll show you how

FRIENDSHIP

Acquaintance

We grew apart
And arguments turned into resentment
Words were lost without respect
No regards for feelings
We began a distant relationship
Where our hearts were stung
With words we could not take back
We were close
We were an exact match
There was a time that I would fight for you
But our egos destroyed what we had
Maybe one day we can reconnect
Touch base on what was
What we used to have
And give our loyalty another try
Maybe not now
But maybe soon
Sometimes I miss our bond
Sometimes I miss you
You held my secrets close
And I held yours too
But the day you crossed me
Told me what I already knew

Maybe not now
But maybe soon…maybe not

Amigos

Sometimes we laugh together
Cry on one another's shoulders
Share precious moments
While surviving in this crazy world
We share a spectacular past with a
different vibe and bond
Too strong is what we are
Personalities blending together
Sometimes we may clash
Sometimes we are fine
But something changed
And we aren't sure why
We find that we live in our own bubbles
Hoping
Praying
Wishing
While the world around us continues to
spin
Sometimes people change and we
aren't told in advance but near the end

Clique

We are strong together
Sharing laughter
Sharing confident vibes
We regret nothing about our circle
This circle that we hold is unique and bold
We sometimes get snippy with one another
And come back together
As if we never broke away
Away from each other
Away and astray

Those beautiful moments that we share
Are great as we can be ourselves
No one demanding that we change
We are life – love – we are above negative change

We all are different in who we are
We rock together close
Thick as thieves
The friendship that we have will continue to be

Sincerely

I want to share these roses with these women, my sisters, my precious friends
Giving each of you something from me
Nothing new and with great comfort
I want you all to know that I care and with this care, sympathy rains upon us
No umbrella to cover our heads
I want to share myself with each of you
These special flowers are only for a few
Hold on tight to the gifts that I give
You all hold my heart
My secrets
My tears
We embrace with a solid hold
We are there for one another
No questions asked
We have given so much to each other
In the present
In the past
Please hold these special flowers
And give them sweet water
A vase to call their own
You all have been my extended family two-fold
Let us continue to walk this path
With love, your friend

MENTAL

Manic

These walls that surround me
Are closing in and are closing in tight
While the depression seeps in
In the middle of the night
Lucid and rapid thoughts
Running wild and free
Passing the baton to no one who can be seen
These thoughts move so fast
No time to gather composure
No time to stop
Too much
While my ego is stroked
My pride is seduced
Can't slow down
Can't hide what isn't new

Depression

It takes your soul
Energy is gone
Strength loses control
Sleep calls after you
Shouting without reason
Each mood is a non-stop demon
Harassing you
Taunting you
Bullying your thoughts
Stealing your happiness
Holding on tight
Giving you spasms that refuse to rest
It makes you cry, scream, and shout
It takes your hunger
It gives quiet to your mouth
Meditation does not help
Counting to ten does not relieve you
Each day is difficult
Harder and harder than before
The pain and the agony
The loss of sensation to live
It greets you by the door
And you have no choice but to let it in
      Unless…

The Panic

One day she stood still
And the weird out-of-body experience
Became engorged and real

Her heart raced
Pumped blood rapidly
Palpitations
Sweat beads

The sick feeling
Of wanting to let her guts go
The true deception of no control

The tremors began
That racing heart with those rapid beats
Legs shaking
Soaked hands and feet

She could not catch her breath
Nor get a grip as reality closed in
It felt like dying
It felt like being burned at the stake
A witch's sin
Breath in and breath out
No words – no hollering – no shouts
The control remains gone
When the "attack" comes along

LOVE
& THE END

Touch

It is simple
Gentle
Quiet
Sensual

It gives chills
Flutters
Butterflies
Peaceful

It gives happiness
Smiles
Glee
Simple joy

It gives release
Tension
Fear
Anxiety

It is simple
Just a…

Broken

He tore her down
      Mentally
      Emotionally
He bypassed her physically
      As he hated bruises that others could see

All the while, not realizing
      That the aura he gave off was negative
      Mean
      Hateful

And one day, she fought back
      Yelling
      Hollering
      Screaming
      Cursing
She swung out her gun
      The one she called Miss Mabel

Shots fired
      Missed his head by inches

He never tore her down again

Unconditional Love

Does it exist?
Do others truly practice this art?
Is it real?
Does it deceive the blind and fall apart?

Does it exist?
Giving off a vibe
That's untouched and not judged

Does it exist?
Beyond the walls
Walls of deceit

Does it exist?
Someone tell me
Please and make it true
Just to touch it
Just to feel it
Make it all gentle and new

Does it exist?
Silence killing the body
As I sit here...
Waiting...needing...

Coffee Shop Love

A simple cup of goodness
A light swirl of cream
A few sugar cubes
The ceramic mugs seducing the steam
Staring into each other's souls
Their hearts beating
Their minds lost in a dream-like control
Adrenaline coursing through their veins
Their lips touch the edge of their mugs
A simple heat
A simple tongue, the warmth beneath
Nothing around them matters
Not now – not ever
A sweet sensational moment
Their hands decide that they should touch…rub…caress
A quiet moment between the two of them
Nothing around them matters in that moment
It's the beginning – something long overdue
A simple love…
     Just those two

Release

He gave her nothing but pain
Heartache
Headache
The words that he spit were so bitter
And without love
And without forgiveness
Her cries…the tears rolled down her face
The sadness, so real, so wretched
And he continued with his foul words
Tongue lashing
Each time she winced with such mental pain
Enough was enough
He made no mends at their table
All lies – all pretending actions of his emotions
She tried to hold on – onto him – onto them
But she was exhausted
And so was her heart
Until one day she spread her wings
Flew high above him
She never looked back

Greek Love

He needs me
Waits for me by the door
I accept all of him
Flaws and all
They test me
They give me struggle on difficult days
I am the one that he has truly loved
The one that is the first to ever see his vulnerable heart
I am the one that if he crosses me, I will break him apart
Piece by piece is what I would do
But I am a gentle scorpion – through and through
He needs me and I am the best
I am the one he should tattoo on his chest
I accepted him when times were tough
I am the one
    The alpha
    The omega
    To his heart
I am the one he will never forget me not

Ready or Not

The years have kept me still and quiet
Longing to begin anew with my
thoughts and words
With the creativity that I knew
Each day, my mind…
Wandered and waited
Pacing with procrastination and delay
I kept my heart at a distance
Too afraid
Too fragile to play
And when the time became the right
moment
I knew that what I held dear is the
strength of my thoughts with my pen
This season and chapter have been
embraced so easily
I became one
I forgot about two
I found my place again…so refreshing
So strong…so true
This time it's different
It will not pass me by
Ready or not, this time, I have to try

-Poetic Mistress
The rebirth of creativity

Made in the USA
Middletown, DE
06 December 2020